Second Series

POTTERY

An Identification and Value Guide

Mariann Katz-Marks

Second Series

MAJOLICA
POTTERY

An Identification and Value Guide

Mariann Katz-Marks

COLLECTOR BOOKS
A Division of Schroeder Publishing Co., Inc.

The current values in this book should be used only as a guide. They are not intended to set prices which vary from one section of the country to another. Auction prices, as well as dealer prices, vary greatly and are affected by conditions as well as demand. Neither the Author nor the Publisher assumes responsibility for any losses that might be incurred as a result of consulting this guide.

Additional copies of this book may be ordered from:

COLLECTOR BOOKS
P.O. Box 3009
Paducah, Kentucky 42001

$9.95 plus $1.00 for postage and handling
Copyright Mariann Katz-Marks 1986
ISBN: 0-89145-312-1

DEDICATION

For Mom, Dad, Ed, Tamara, Irene and Alice.

ACKNOWLEDGMENTS

I wish to thank all the members of my family who contributed, each in his own way, to the completion of this book. My parents, Alice B. Katz and Robert W. Katz Sr. have provided me with the atmosphere in which creativity could flourish, and have been most supportive in all my endeavors.

I also wish to thank my husband, Edward O.C. Marks, for his tremendous support of these projects as well as for the original idea to write a book about Majolica.

I especially appreciate all the help and encouragement given by my three daughters, Tamara, Irene, and Alice.

In addition, I would like to thank:
    Robert W. Katz, Jr. and Deborah H. Katz
    James E. Katz
    Mrs. Edward O.C. Marks, Sr.
    RaeDell Marks

TABLE OF CONTENTS

INTRODUCTION

I am glad to be able to present another book of photographs of Victorian Majolica. All of the letters and comments on my first book were greatly appreciated. So many of you were happy to find pictures of pieces in your own collections and perhaps to discover the name of the potter or the year of manufacture.

I hope that this new book with more color photos and descriptions will add to your knowledge of your own collections. Those of us who have handled a great many pieces of this Victorian pottery are always amazed as new patterns are constantly encountered.

Collecting Habits

Some collectors find that eventually they wish to specialize in one type of Majolica. For many, this is English Majolica. Almost all the well known manufacturers are represented including Wedgwood, Minton, George Jones, and Holdcroft. The works by these four English potteries probably comprise the greatest number of items of beauty and value. There are also many English pieces that cannot be readily attributed to the famous potters, but are very desirable in any collection. In general, the English pieces tend to be more colorful and finely detailed, adding to their value.

Another popular collecting area is Etruscan Majolica made by the Pennsylvania firm of Griffin, Smith and Hill. These are highly sought after and the series contains some very valuable and beautiful pieces. There are many collectors in the United States who have limited their collection to works only by this manufacturer. Within that group, there are some who exclusively collect the very popular "Shell & Seaweed" pattern. Others try to find one example of each pattern made by Griffin, Smith and Hill, and still others try to obtain every design in all sizes and colors. A collection of Majolica such as that, can number into the hundreds.

Perhaps by far the greatest number of Majolica collectors do not limit their collections in any way, trying to include desirable pieces by any potter from any country. These include items made in Germany, Austria, France, and Czechoslovakia, among others. Most·of these are not truly of the Victorian period, but many collections are extended to include lead glazed pottery of a naturalistic design no matter what the date of manufacture. This would include the great body of interesting figural pitchers, particularly the mouth-pouring variety which can form an outstanding collection in themselves.

The best advice I can give on how to structure your collection is to buy what appeals to you individually. This makes the most interesting and attractive display. A variety of colors and forms will strengthen any grouping.

The price ranges given in this book were taken from sales at antique shows and reported auction results. I tried to give a general range from low to high that would account for differences across the country. Please remember that prices tend to be higher in areas where Majolica is difficult to obtain and where many people are looking for it. In areas of the country where it is less well known, you may find greater bargains. The prices given are for items in generally good condition. Almost all Majolica has some evidence of its age and the glaze will have picked up small imperfections. In addition, many pieces started life with some "in the kiln" imperfections, as it was not manufactured as carefully as fine porcelain. Majolica was made inexpensively enough to be used on a daily basis by the average household of the Victorian period.

I hope you will enjoy looking through these photographs as much as I enjoyed taking them. Each of these works of art has it's own place in the history of 19th C. pottery and is a tribute to the innovative and creative potters that produced them.

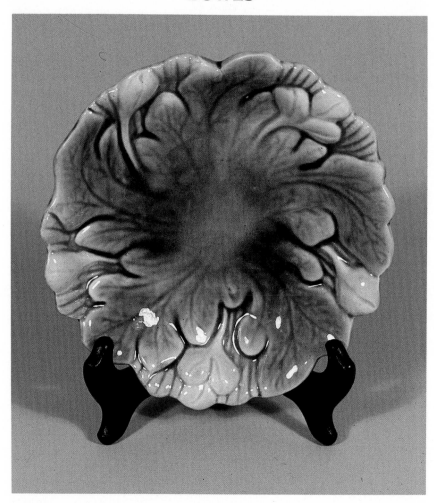

ETRUSCAN B4 LEAF DISH—6″d. This little dish in attractive tones of green, brown and yellow is difficult to find. I have had just this one. It can be found in other color combinations. $75.00-110.00.

WEDGEWOOD FAN AND PRUNUS SMALL DISH—6½"d. This abstract fan pattern compliments the larger rendition of the design to be found on the bird and fan pieces. Marked Wedgwood. $65.00-75.00.

LUGGAGE STRAP, CABBAGE LEAF AND FLORAL BOWL—12″l. Identical in every respect to the basket pictured in my first book except this one was designed without the handle for use as a bowl. Such a beautiful and unusual design – the Victorian potters were famous for their flights of whimsy. $275.00-375.00.

GEORGE JONES BIRD ON EDGE OF BOWL 7″d. A beautiful example of his way with birds; this little one is poised for flight on the edge of a beautiful turquoise dish supported on a thick twisted vine. Lovely holly leaves and berries complete the motif. A jewel! $350.00-450.00.

MINTONS CUPID COMPOTE, 6½"h. Graceful and classic interpretation of the cupid theme; they support the oval lobed compote on their wings with two kissing doves in the central area adding an unusual touch. Signed MINTONS with the number 930 and the year mark for 1875. $750.00-850.00.

GEORGE JONES TRIPLE LOBED LEAF RELISH SERVER. 12"l. Graceful white dogwood with a branch handle display George Jones' expertise using simple elements from nature. His pieces have a sophisticated grace almost unparalleled by any other potter except Minton. $325.00-425.00.

WEDGWOOD OVAL CENTERPIECE BOWL WITH LEAFY GARLAND. 15″l.
This bowl incorporates a beautiful cobalt blue base with yellow wicker basket
work around the top. The graceful drape of the garland is accented with pink
ribbons. Signed Wedgwood. $450.00-650.00.

GEORGE JONES BACCHANAL COMPOTE. 6″l. This diminutive compote
could grace the serving table at your next wine party. Two cherubs hold the
small bowl aloft, each lying on a goatskin bulging with wine. $300.00-395.00.

HOLDCROFT SHELL-SHAPED BOWL. 9″d. Finely detailed bowl, held slightly aloft on shell-shaped feet. Signed Holdcroft. $100.00-145.00.

ETRUSCAN MORNING GLORY COMPOTE. 8″d. This hard-to-find compote does not usually turn up in very good condition. I have seen them signed and unsigned, and with a very rare, bright red background. This example, in mint condition, $250.00-295.00.

HOLDCROFT SHELL ON PEDESTAL. 8″h. Very well done with nice nautical detailing on the pedestal. Signed Holdcroft. $250.00-295.00.

GEORGE JONES SMALL OVAL GRAPE PATTERN BOWL. 6″l. Unsigned but unmistakably Jones; part of his Bacchanalian series; the feet are gnarled grape vines. $125.00-195.00.

WEDGWOOD ROUND CENTERPIECE BOWL. 12″d. Beautiful example of Wedgwood's attention to detail, the garland is encrusted with flowers and wrapped with ribbon. Yellow wicker detailing on the top. $500.00-600.00.

WEDGWOOD OVAL BASKETWEAVE AND GRAPE LEAF BOWL. 12″d. This pretty piece has such delicate handles in the shape of gnarled grape vines. Caution is advised when purchasing this – I have had them with broken handles which have been re-glued. It is a very hard piece to find in perfect condition. Still very beautiful and worthwhile even with imperfections! Look for this also with a white background instead of the cobalt. $250.00-295.00.

WEDGWOOD BIRD PERCHING ON EDGE OF DISH. 7″d. The delicate beauty of this is hard to believe; the little bird is poised over a group of white pond lilies floating on a cobalt blue dish. A rare piece which I have seen only once. $375.00-425.00.

UNUSUAL SIX-SIDED BOWL. 15″l. Turquoise basketweave and pink prunus blossoms decorate the body of this unusual six-sided bowl. Lovely rich lavender lining. $225.00-250.00.

GEORGE JONES DOGWOOD BOWL. 6″d. This bowl is part of Jones' dogwood series, a large group including cheese keepers and pitchers. A charming detail is the addition of twisted branch feet. $325.00-365.00.

GEORGE JONES MONUMENTAL SHELL BOWL ON PEDESTAL. 13″d. This piece is large and with unbelievable beauty and detail. The pinks are astounding and the detail on the base is so well done. The shell is supported above the base on a nest of white coral. Worthy of a central place in anyone's collection. $1200.00-1500.00.

HOLDCROFT POND LILY BOWL. 8″d. A nice little bowl which utilizes the pretty combination of browns and greens so typical of Victorian Majolica. $75.00-95.00.

MINTON RABBIT CENTERPIECE. 8″l. This piece is truly desirable from every aspect with these wonderful little bunnies crouching under the turquoise cabbage leaf surrounded by foliage. Whimsical pieces such as this are most desirable to many collectors. $950.00-1250.00.

ETRUSCAN SHELL FRUIT DISH. 5″d. This little dish belongs to the large family of Griffin, Smith, & Hill's shell & seaweed series. $95.00-125.00.

WEDGWOOD FRUIT BOWL. 8″d. Wedgwood's distinctive taupe, rose and yellow coloring is put to good use in this bowl designed to hold strawberries. $110.00-135.00.

ETRUSCAN SHELL & SEAWEED CAKE STAND. 9″d. A rare piece, and one hard to find in good condition. I have never seen one without repair, which of course is perfectly acceptable in rare pieces. These must have been used very frequently in the Victorian household. $300.00-350.00.

MINTON SIX-LOBED WATER LILY SERVING BOWL 9″d. Minton displays ingenuity again with pond lilies in this attractive tiered relish server with small lily buds protruding from under the three larger leaves. One central figural flower serves as a handle. $200.00-250.00.

PIECES WITH COVERS

ROPE EDGE SARDINE BOX 8″l. This sardine box is attractive in the more rustic style, as opposed to the finely detailed pieces of the major English potters, eg. Jones, Minton, & Wedgwood. Most Majolica falls into the rustic category. $250.00-300.00.

HOLDCROFT POND LILY SARDINE BOX. 8″l. This is one of the more unusual boxes. The detail of the little fish swimming on the side adds interest as do the pretty white lily buds on each corner. The fish are particularly realistic. This is the only sardine by Holdcroft I have been able to photograph, although other designs must exist. $300.00-350.00.

CHILD ON CLOTHES TRUNK TOBACCO BOX. 6″l. A boy lies atop a large
clothing trunk eating a huge slice of pink watermelon. Although the boy is
American, the box was made in Austria and is unusual. Austrian tobacco boxes
usually portray figural animals. Desirable for collectors of tobacco boxes, Majolica, and figurals. $225.00-265.00.

FLORAL AND FENCE SARDINE BOX. 7″l. Most sardine boxes are decorated
with various types of fish, so this nice floral rendition is refreshingly different.
Bowls can also be found in this pattern. The turquoise area represents a picket
fence. $175.00-225.00.

HERON CHEESE KEEPER. 11"h. I thought this was one of the nicest cheesekeepers I had ever seen. It was not made in the "Wedgwood" school of pottery but by one of the less well known English potters whose name at this time is still a mystery. For them, this was a major piece and much attention to detail can be seen in the lovely cattails, and in the lavish coloring of the bird. Look at the gracefulness of this large heron with his catch for the day clasped in his beak! He is standing in a bed of pond lilies outlined with bamboo. This piece is very representative of what is so appealing about Majolica. $1200.00-1500.00.

ETRUSCAN SHELL & SEAWEED BUTTER DISH. 4"h. This one is rare and desirable and may take awhile to find to complete your shell and seaweed collection. I have been fortunate enough to have had two. It also comes in another variation with a different arrangement of shells on the cover. Expect to pay in the $300.00-395.00 range.

GEORGE JONES MATCH BOX WITH STRIKER ON BOTTOM. 4"l. This diminutive piece has the George Jones signature seal on the underside of the lid and the underside of the base is ridged to be used as a striker. Most unusual. $245.00-275.00.

HOLDCROFT POND LILY CHEESE KEEPER. 9"h. Especially beautiful coloration, the white lilies seem to float on the green lily leaves. The handle is one beautiful lily bud. I have seen it in two sizes. This is the smaller one. $350.00-450.00.

HOLDCROFT OAK LEAF CHEESE KEEPER. 5"h. This one is much smaller than usual, and the motif is kept very simple. Still, it is appealing and pretty with a nice figural handle. $110.00-125.00.

WEDGWOOD RABBIT GAME DISH. 7"l. A nice example of Wedgwood's use of the classic Majolica colors of green and brown – the rabbit crouches atop the dish. Around the base are representations of various game animals surrounded by garlands of greenery. The Wedgwood pottery was particularly fond of various types of garlands. This is the small one. It came also in a larger size. $850.00-950.00.

GEORGE JONES DAISY AND FENCE CHEESE KEEPER. 11″h. For those who love George Jones Majolica (I never met a collector who did not like the work of this pottery), this stupendous cheese keeper will be the centerpiece of the collection. The cobalt blue background is particularly effective. Everything about this large and beautiful piece is ideal. $2000.00-2500.00.

MINTON GAME DISH. 12″l. This Minton game dish is a very desirable piece, has a large sculptured hare and mallard duck on the lid. The base is a realistic brown basketweave with graceful oak leaves. $1500.00-2000.00.

GEORGE JONES QUAIL AND RABBIT GAME DISH. 12″l. I know I will not be able to do justice to this piece with mere words. The picture speaks for itself. I must say that this is a personal favorite and a good example for students of Majolica; it demonstrates all the elements that go into making a very valuable addition to one's collection. $2750.00-3000.00.

ETRUSCAN SARDINE BOX. 6″l. Try to add this to your Etruscan collection if you can find it. I have also seen it with a different color background. The design is almost identical to the George Jones sardine box, although here the more rustic modeling and the Etruscan coloration is unmistakable. $450.00-550.00.

WEDGWOOD CHEESE KEEPER. 10"h. Yellow floral and green leaf cheese keeper with a brown basketweave base. Any cheese keeper is hard to find but those by Wedgwood are particularly scarce. $395.00-495.00.

ROPE AND FERN CHEESE KEEPER LID. 8"h. Such a pretty lid with it's lavender background stands on it's own without the base. I always pick up these odd lids and bases when I can; I have actually put them together years after the purchase of individual components. The price for the lid only, $150.00-195.00.

SHELL FINIAL SARDINE BOX. 7"l. I had never seen this one before. The coloring is very pleasant and the big shell finial adds value. $275.00-325.00.

WEDGWOOD BOAT SARDINE BOX. 9"l. I have also had this with a white background. It has the words "Sardinia" impressed on the side. Outstanding about this is it's figural boat shape with fishnet draping down each side. $350.00-450.00.

WEDGWOOD BOAT SARDINE BOX. 8″l. Here is the same sardine in the white striped version. $350.00-450.00.

GEORGE JONES DOGWOOD CHEESE KEEPER. 10″h. Slightly smaller and more squat than most cheese keepers, this belongs to George Jones' large series of dogwood pieces. The design also occurs in pitchers, larger cheese keepers, plates, etc. $450.00-550.00.

ETRUSCAN ALBINO OAK SOAP BOX. 6"l. I feel so fortunate to have had this in my possession for a short time and to have photographed it for this book. I know this has to be among the rarest of Majolica. The oak soap box is a great rarity in the Etruscan series, but this one is even more unusual because it is done in the albino coloration. Among albino pieces, this is also a rarity because it utilizes three shades of luster, a pale yellow, a deeper saffron, and a beautiful shade of pink. There is a liner inside. Signed. $500.00.

PITCHERS

FIELDING FIGURAL SHELL PITCHER. 8″h. The body of this graceful piece represents a figural shell, with ocean waves splashing at the base, quite a beautiful form. Pitchers such as this with a figural quality are particularly desirable. $275.00-325.00.

HONEY BEAR FIGURAL PITCHER. 9"h. This amusing bear belongs to the family of mouth-pouring pitchers. The handle forms a spoon. $250.00-295.00.

ETRUSCAN CORN PITCHER. 6″h. Another Etruscan rarity made by a famous American pottery of the 19th century, Griffin, Smith & Hill. $275.00-350.00.

DOGWOOD ON BARK OVAL PITCHER. 8"h. This pretty oval shaped pitcher was unsigned but the colors are in imitation of Wedgwood. You will notice the distinctive taupe color on the handle and branches. $150.00-195.00.

CHICKENS WITH WHEAT SHEAF PITCHER. 7"h. This wonderful piece portrays two chickens going around a sheaf of wheat – a good example of how amusing and whimsical Majolica motifs can be. Probably English. $250.00-275.00.

COBALT FLORAL PITCHER. 8″h. This combination of colors is very desirable – cobalt, pinks, greens & yellows. $125.00-150.00.

BUTTERFLY LIP FLORAL PITCHER. 7"h. The design of this is so similar to the Etruscan butterfly lip pitcher. This is either a forerunner or copy by an unknown potter. $125.00-150.00.

ETRUSCAN CORAL CREAM PITCHER. 3½"h. Griffin, Smith & Hill made these little pitchers in a variety of sizes. They are all hard to find. $150.00-200.00.

MONKEY FIGURAL PITCHER. 9″h. I just love these pitchers. I have had them in 8″, 7″ and 5″ sizes as well, all with a lavender lining. Scarce! $325.00-350.00.

GREEN LEAF SYRUP PITCHER. 4"h. Attractive earth tones and a nice shape give this little one value. $125.00-145.00.

MINTON PITCHER. 8"h. This piece is distinguished by its intensity of coloring and simplicity of design. Most Minton pieces have more elaborate decoration, however this is very appealing nonetheless. $225.00-250.00.

ENGLISH ROSE PITCHER. 6"h. Cobalt coloring adds to the beauty of this
English pitcher. $110.00-125.00.

BIRDS AND NEST PITCHER. 7"h. This birds nest has the eggs already hat-
ched! Also look for a version with unhatched eggs. $125.00-150.00.

HOLDCROFT DOGWOOD SYRUP PITCHER. 4″ h. This is a tiny version of the larger Holdcroft dogwood pitchers. $125.00-150.00.

BUTTERFLY AND BAMBOO CREAM PITCHER. 3″h. This little cream pitcher utilizes the butterfly theme to full effect, surrounding it with a frame of bamboo. $110.00-145.00.

MINTON COURT JESTER JUG. 13″h. This splended and imposing piece uses the court jester as a finial. The body displays various figures along with grape motifs; most certainly a jug for serving wine. $450.00-550.00.

GEORGE JONES UNDERWATER PITCHER. 8″h. The small band at the top represents the sky with gulls soaring overhead. Underneath are a variety of fish, crabs and underwater plant life! Quite a display and a very attractive piece. $325.00-375.00.

HOLDCROFT DOGWOOD PITCHER. 9″h. The coloring on this one is very
nice. These also came with a white background. $175.00-225.00.

ETRUSCAN BASEBALL AND SOCCER PLAYERS JUG IN FULL COLOR.
7¾"h. This Griffin, Smith & Hill jug is among the most rare of all the Etruscan
series. Modeled in the manner of a Wedgwood jug, it displays the particularly American sport of baseball – the Wedgwood jug portrays cricket players.
This example is signed. Extremely rare in multi-color with the GSH mark.
$1200.00-1500.00.

ETRUSCAN ALBINO CORAL SYRUP PITCHER. 7″h. Another rare and unusual Etruscan piece. The albino decoration is quite well done here. Usually it is not as colorful. This price for the more colorful albino example is $250.00-300.00.

SAMUEL LEAR SUNFLOWER AND CLASSICAL URN SYRUP PITCHER.
8″h. Here is the pretty Samuel Lear sunflower design done in a tin-topped pitcher. $150.00-200.00.

IVY ON TREE BARK PITCHER. 8″h. Simply done interpretation with the classic browns and greens. English. $110.00-125.00.

PLATES AND PLATTERS

OYSTER PLATE. 9″d. $65.00-75.00.

PICKET FENCE AND MORNING GLORY DEEP DISH. 7″d. A picket fence pattern surrounds the mottled center. $65.00-85.00.

MINTON WATER LILY PLATE. 9″d. This restrained interpretation of the classic water lily theme is so effective. This set consisted of twelve plates and one huge platter. Each plate, $95.00. The platter, $300.00.

WEDGWOOD CRANE PLATE. 9″d. A reticulated edge with simulated basketweave, as well as the long necked crane, distinguishes this plate. $150.00-175.00.

OVAL GERANIUM RELISH TRAY. 8″l. The colors here are so similar to Wedgwood. However, I believe it may be American, probably Clifton by Chesapeake Pottery Co. $65.00-75.00.

BEGONIA LEAF PLATTER. 14″l. Open handles and a central begonia flower form the main motif. $75.00-110.00.

LOBE-EDGED MORNING GLORY PLATE. 9″d. $75.00-95.00.

HOLDCROFT FISH AND DAISY PLATE. 9″d. This nice fish also appears on plates with a turquoise background. $95.00-125.00.

WEDGWOOD FISH PLATE. 9″d. $125.00-150.00.

FISH PLATTER. 14″l. An unusual shape and well placed fish distinguish this piece. Definitely English. $225.00-265.00.

BEGONIA LEAF PLATTER. 13"l. $110.00-135.00.

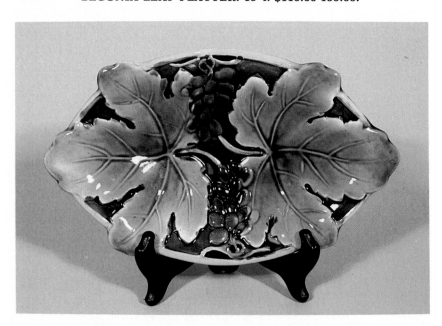

GRAPE LEAF RELISH TRAY. 8"l. $85.00-110.00.

SWAN HANDLED PLATTER. 13"l. If you look closely, you can see that the handles are swans with wings outstretched – a very beautiful variation on a bird theme! $175.00-200.00.

HOLDCROFT DOGWOOD PLATE. 8"d. $65.00-85.00.

GEORGE JONES PALM AND GRAPELEAF TRAY. 8"d. The colors on this are spectacular – a lovely small tray by George Jones. $225.00-275.00.

BLACKBERRY PLATTER. 14"l. $125.00-145.00.

OYSTER PLATE. 9″d. $76.00-95.00.

MINTON OYSTER PLATE 10″d. A deep cobalt mottling marks this handsome piece. $175.00-225.00.

MINTON OYSTER PLATE. 10″d. Here is the same plate in a different coloration with turquoise. $150.00-200.00.

GEORGE JONES WATER LILY PLATE. 8″d. These are fun to collect in sets; if you search diligently you may be able to find the matching cakestand. $85.00-100.00.

WEDGWOOD ONION & PICKLE RELISH TRAY. 8″l. $175.00-200.00.

LEAF PLATTER. 13″l. $95.00-125.00.

FLORAL AND BASKETWEAVE PLATTER. 11″l. $110.00-125.00.

GEORGE JONES TRIVET. 7″d. This is an attractive trivet in Jones' colors. $85.00-95.00.

WHITE LILAC OVAL LOBED PLATTER. 13"d. $110.00-125.00.

HOLDCROFT WATER LILY PLATTER AND INDIVIDUAL DISHES. 14" platter and 6" dishes. Holdcroft marked this set with his signature. Stylistic water lilies grace the handles and a thin bamboo rim surrounds all the pieces in the set. $325.00 for the platter and set of 8 dishes.

MINTON ROUND STRAWBERRY SERVING DISH. 9"d. Outstanding coloration marks this pretty strawberry dish. I believe these were intended as individual servers to be placed in front of every dinner guest at dessert time. The larger type with sugar and cream inserts were to be used in the center of the table. $285.00-325.00.

GEORGE JONES OYSTER PLATE WITH FIGURAL SHELL. 10"d. The remarkable thing about this is the center shell which is raised. $200.00-225.00.

WEDGWOOD SWIMMING SEAL PLATTER. 17". A nice addition to Wedgwood's nautical themes is this whimsical platter with seals frolicking amid the ocean waves. $225.00-275.00.

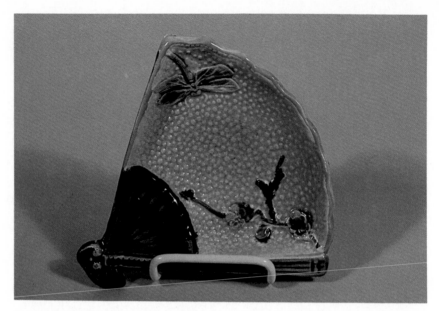

FAN SHAPED DISH. 6"d. A dragonfly swoops in on a prunus branch; these are fun to collect in sets. Watch for different background colors – it is attractive to mix the colors and use them for side dishes at the table. $40.00-50.00.

HOLDCROFT WATER LILY PLATE. 8"d. The coloration here is elegantly simple and the graceful lines quite effective. Despite it's simple theme, this was one of my favorite plates for a long time. $75.00-85.00.

FIELDING FAN OYSTER PLATE. 9″d. Here is an unusual one for either Majolica or oyster plate collectors. It is signed Fielding, and has a nice combination of colors and design. Each indentation for an oyster is an oriental fan. $185.00-225.00.

WEDGWOOD DOLPHIN OYSTER PLATE. 9″d. Quite a gaudy and effective departure for Wedgwood. There is a dolphin between each shell. Of course, the swirls represent waves. $185.00-225.00.

ETRUSCAN APPLE AND STRAWBERRY PLATE. 9″d. This particular plate was one of the first pieces of Majolica I every bought and it remains a favorite to this day. Look also for background colors of pink and blue. $95.00-110.00.

GEOMETRIC PLATTER WITH STRIPES AND DAISY HANDLES. 13″l. $110.00-125.00.

FAN CAKE STAND. 9″d. I have had this pattern in a plate but had never seen it in a low cake stand! $110.00-135.00.

ETRUSCAN OAK LEAF BREAD TRAY. 13″d. The large oak leaf bread tray used to be fairly common to find but now I hardly ever see one. Look for nice bright pink edge coloration and good condition. They are especially hard to find in good shape. Check the handle for repair. I have even seen them for sale with the handle completely broken off. $85.00-125.00.

WEDGWOOD BASKETWEAVE CLOTH ON BREAD TRAY. 12"d. A realistic rendition of a breadcloth lays across this pretty tray. $200.00-225.00.

FERN AND FLORAL PLATE. 8"d. $75.00-85.00.

WEDGWOOD ONION AND PICKLE RELISH TRAY. 8″l. $110.00-125.00.

ROUND ALBINO DISH. 9½″d. Unusual albino coloration on a serrated edged dish with open handle. $20.00-25.00.

WEDGWOOD MINIATURE OYSTER PLATE. 7"d. This is much smaller than the usual oyster plate; effective coloration with the dark blue of the ocean waves. $150.00-175.00.

WEDGWOOD SHELL PLATE. 9"d. This plate is part of a larger set which included a platter. Coloration will vary. $110.00-125.00.

HOLDCROFT CATTAIL AND FISH PLATTER. 25″ l. I am sure Holdcroft was proud to place his signature on this masterful fish platter. The edges have large figural cattails. $350.00-450.00.

WEDGWOOD SHELL FISH PLATTER. 23″l. This is one of the most beautiful pieces of Wedgwood I have seen. It can also be found with a white background. $350.00-395.00.

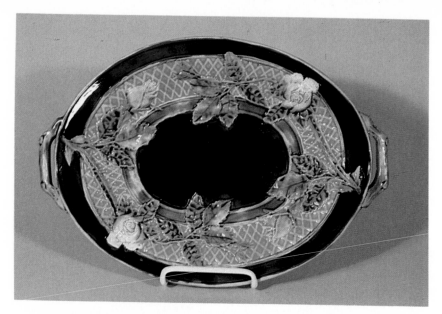

ROSE ON BASKETWEAVE PLATTER. 13"d. $110.00-135.00.

TWIN SHELL ON WAVES BREAD TRAY. 14"l. $175.00-195.00.

WEDGWOOD SHELL DISH. 6"d. $45.00-65.00.

BOW ON BASKETWEAVE PLATE. 6"d. This plate is part of a larger set which included a large platter and a teaset. $55.00-65.00.

SUNFLOWER OYSTER PLATE. 10"d. Another unusual oyster plate, this time with sunflowers in the indentations. $125.00-145.00.

MORNING GLORY AND PICKET FENCH DISH. 9"d. A deep plate or dish with an attractive fence pattern. $65.00-85.00.

BARREL STAVES AND FLORAL PLATTER. 10"d. $110.00-145.00.

TEA SERVICE

FLORAL AND BASKETWEAVE TEAPOT. 4½"h. The metal lid adds to the value of this teapot. $125.00-145.00.

LEAF AND BOW SUGAR BOWL. 4"h. See the companion cream pitcher on page 123 of my first book, *Majolica Pottery*. $55.00-75.00.

IVY COVERED COTTAGE SUGAR BOWL AND CREAM PITCHER. 4"h. 3"h. This unusual figural design also comes in a teapot. $75.00-95.00 for the covered sugar bowl and $75.00-110.00 for the cream pitcher. The pitcher comes in more than one size.

HOLLY AND BERRIES TEAPOT. 6"h. This design includes a bark spout and handle. $145.00-175.00.

SAMUEL LEAR SUNFLOWER AND CLASSICAL URN TEAPOT. 6″h. This teapot joins a large family of pieces in the urn and sunflower pattern. $175.00-210.00.

ISLE OF MAN THREE-LEGGED FIGURAL TEAPOT. 8″h. This very unusual piece is in the shape of a three-legged man. The head lifts off to pour in the water and the tea pours through the leg at the back. It is marked "W. BROUGHTON, SO. DUKE ST. DOUGLAS." It seems to have been an advertising piece. "Douglas" is the capital of the ISLE OF MAN, which is located off Great Britain in the Irish Sea. This piece has value from an historical perspective, and as a desirable lidded figural piece. $550.00-650.00.

FLORAL AND BASKETWEAVE TEAPOT. 5"h. $125.00-145.00.

MINTON MONKEY FIGURAL TEAPOT. 7"h. A desirable Minton figural piece. $525.00-625.00.

HOLDCROFT CHINAMAN ON A COCONUT TEAPOT. 7"h. This could either be a melon or coconut. The chinaman's head comes off to reveal the opening for the water. Any of these figural teapots are rare and valuable. $395.00-425.00.

HOLDCROFT MELON SUGAR BOWL AND CREAM PITCHER. 4"h. 2"h. These match the pattern on the teapot in my first book, page 128. The background color on the teapot is brown and these can probably be found also in that color. $75.00-95.00 each.

WARDLE BAMBOO AND FERN MUSTACHE CUP AND SAUCER. 7″d. This is a beautiful example of a rare mustache cup. The lavender lining is particularly nice. $225.00-275.00.

MINTON'S CHINAMAN TEAPOT. 6″h. Another lovely example of Minton's way with figurals. Again, here the head lifts off. $525.00-625.00.

ETRUSCAN SHELL AND SEAWEED MUSTACHE CUP. 8″d. A rare find! Be careful that you also get the large 8″ saucer which is the correct size. Of course, even without the saucer, it is not an item to be passed up. $275.00-295.00 complete with the saucer.

ETRUSCAN CAULIFLOWER CUP AND SAUCER. 7″d. This cup and saucer is part of the Etruscan cauliflower series which also includes a teaset and two sizes of plates. The set pictured is very rare. They will likely be the last pieces of the set to be found. $175.00-200.00.

PINEAPPLE CUP AND SAUCER. 7"d. Look for other pieces in the pineapple series, such as the teaset and various size plates. $95.00-110.00.

CLASSICAL HARP VASE. 6″h. A very graceful harp with classical woman forms a small bud vase. $110.00-145.00.

LILAC THROATED SONG BIRD VASES. 6″h. What could be prettier than these two little birds and their trumpet-shaped flowers forming a bud vase! $225.00-265.00 the pair.

TRIPLET HANDLED URN GROUP. 5 to 7″h. Each in this lovely trio has an intense turquoise lining. They are unsigned, but the coloring is so reminiscent of Brownfield. $175.00-200.00 for all three.

PINEAPPLE HAND VASE. 13″h. If you compare this to the vase on page 131 of my previous book, you will notice that this has much more detail. The size also, is just stupendous – this has to been seen to be believed. Notice the tassel at the wrist and the ring on the finger. English registry mark. $450.00-550.00.

THOMAS SHIRLEY RAM HEAD VASE. 6"h. This one is unsigned, but you just can't miss the workmanship and colors of Thomas Shirley, ca. 1850. $85.00-110.00.

GEORGE JONES CLASSICAL PUTTI VASES. 8″h. Lilac drapery enhances
this classical pair balancing bud vases on their heads. $350.00-450.00 for the
pair.

GEORGE JONES CLASSICAL PUTTI WITH NAUTILUS SHELLS AND
VASES. 6″h. Here is another pair of George Jones' putti, this time in a nautical
setting! $350.00-450.00 for the pair.

RARE AND UNUSUAL CRANE AND PRUNUS VASE. 6″h. There is always an exception to every rule! The second photo shows the back with it's applied flowers. We like to say that true Victorian Majolica does not *usually* have applied decoration such as flowers. Quite rare. $125.00-150.00.

SONGBIRD WITH TRIPLE THROATED VASE. 8″h. $195.00-225.00.

BIRD ON TREE BRANCH. 7"h. $125.00-150.00.

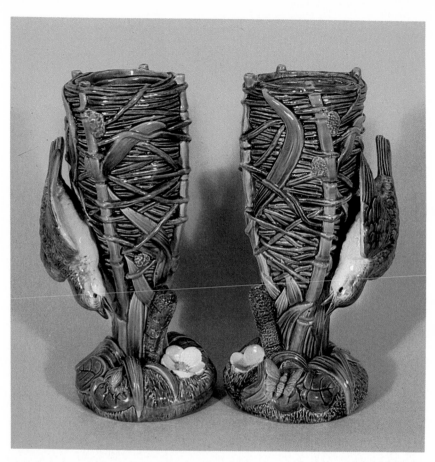

GEORGE JONES BIRD'S NEST AND BIRD VASES. 8"h. These are truly the most outstanding pair of Jones vases! The detail in the bird's nests is unbelievable. One of these alone is worth approximately $375.00-425.00, and about $800.00 for the very special pair.

FLORAL AND BASKETWEAVE CUSPIDOR. 7"h. $125.00-150.00.

UNUSUAL FLORAL SOAP DISH. 4″d. This is molded in one piece and there is a small hole for the water to drain out. $85.00-110.00.

GEORGE JONES FLORAL STRAWBERRY SERVING DISH. 10″d. Two figural
flowers form the cups for sugar. $295.00-350.00.

ETRUSCAN SUNFLOWER CUSPIDOR. 7"h. This is a very rare Etruscan
piece. The sunflower cupsidor was also produced with a blue background.
$450.00-500.00.

HOLDCROFT DRUMMER BOY MATCH HOLDER. 3"h. A uniquely design-
ed piece by Holdcroft; the bottom of one upturned foot is ridged for a match
striker. $250.00-295.00.

ETRUSCAN SHELL AND SEAWEED CUSPIDOR. 7"h. Another one of the rare Etruscan cuspidors; this one will be needed for cuspidor collections in general and to complete shell & seaweed collections as well. $500.00-595.00.

GEORGE JONES EGYPTIAN STYLE PLANTER. 7"h. The cobalt blue coloring and the stately geometric Egyptian motif sets this apart from most Jones pieces. $450.00-550.00.

FAN SPOON HOLDER. 5″h. $65.00-85.00.

GEORGE JONES STRAWBERRY SERVER WITH SPOON. 13″l. This has two separate inserts, one for cream and one for sugar. The serving spoon is very rare. $550.00-650.00.

MINTON CATTAIL PLANTER WITH UNDER DISH. 6″h. A beautifully simple piece with lavish coloring. $295.00-350.00.

MORNING GLORY EGG BASKET WITH EGG CUPS. 6″h. Egg baskets are hard to find, particularly with all the egg cups intact. $250.00-295.00.

HOLDCROFT ARTIST-SIGNED MONUMENTAL BIRD UMBRELLA STAND. Approximately three feet tall. This extraordinary piece is unbelievable. The bird is just huge and the detailing extremely fine. It is signed by the artist near the base, "T. Fay, Sculptor". $2000.00.

MINTON SAILOR BOY SWEETMEAT DISH. 6″h. This is part of a large group
of figural Minton dishes. $235.00-265.00.

GEORGE JONES DAISY AND BANANA LEAF PLANTER. 10"h. This has a lovely lavender lining. Also look for a cheese keeper and umbrella stand in this pattern. $375.00-425.00.

FLORAL AND FERN PLANTER WITH GROTESQUE HEADS. 7"h. Unsigned and unusual. $175.00-210.00.

MINTON PUTTI CARRYING SHELL. 8″h. Fine detail and graceful forms distinguish this lovely Minton sculpture. $495.00-995.00.

WEDGWOOD FIGURAL CANDLESTICKS. 11″h. These are very rare and very beautiful; the value is enhanced because they are a pair. $650.00-850.00.

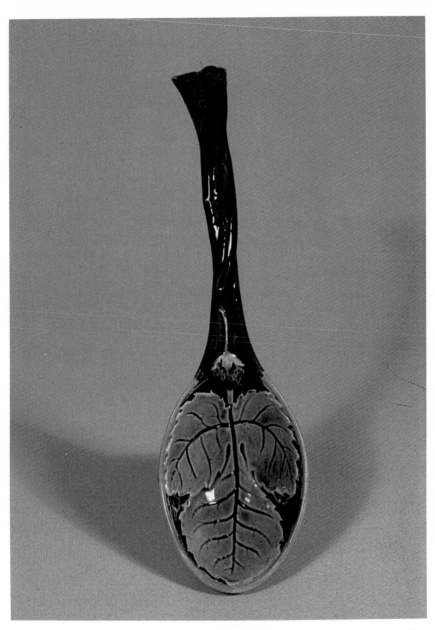

HOLDCROFT STRAWBERRY SERVING SPOON. 5″l. These spoons originally went with the strawberry servers—very hard to find. $175.00-225.00.

COBALT JARDINAIRE WITH GROTESQUE HEADS. 8″h. A lavender lining and effectively used coloration make this a striking piece. $250.00-295.00.

MINTON BOY AND GIRL WITH SHELLS. 8″h. $300.00-395.00.

BOY RIDING A GOAT. 9"h. The sculptural quality and flowing lines of this figure are just beautiful. Unsigned, but it is certainly by one of the major English potters. $325.00-395.00.

WORCESTER DOLPHIN CANDLESTICK. 4"h. Notice the similarity to the Worcester piece on page 24 of my first book. Worcester Majolica is very hard to find. The coloration and the intensity of the glaze is a little different from most Victorian Majolica. $250.00-295.00.

WEDGWOOD WINE COOLER. 10"h. This can be quite a useful and decorative table accent. $300.00-350.00.

WEDGWOOD BLACKBERRY JARDINARIE. 10"h. Wedgwood called this the "Bramble" garden pot. It was modeled by Birks and registered in 1868. $350.00-395.00.

GEORGE JONES STRAWBERRY SERVER. 10″d. This is a graceful treatment of the classic theme. It is unusual for the single cup to be attached to the center of the bowl. $395.00-425.00.

PICKET FENCE AND RASBERRY PATTERN PLANTER. 8″h. Lavender lining. $250.00-295.00.

GEORGE JONES WINE CADDY. 13″l. This is certainly one of the most elaborate and intricate Jones pieces. The wheels are attached to a spoke, and actually turn! The sides of the wine holders are reticulated with realistic grape leaves and the little putto in the center is eating a bunch of grapes. $2000.00-2500.00.

WEDGWOOD SALT DIP. 5″h. A small child holds a wicker basket. $235.00-265.00.

TENUOUS MAJOLICA SHELL CUSPIDOR. 5"h. Although it is not as gaily colored as most Victorian Majolica, this cuspidor is among the rarest of American Majolica. I never thought I would see a piece with the elusive "TENUOUS MAJOLICA" mark, but here it is. See the photo of the mark at the end of the book. $225.00-265.00.

FLORAL MUG. 4"h. $65.00-75.00.

MINTON TWIN BIRD INK WELL. 9"l. Surely this is a lovely and valuable piece by Minton. Each little bird's head lifts to reveal the inkwells. $350.00-425.00.

FLORAL CUSPIDOR. 7"h. $175.00-200.00.

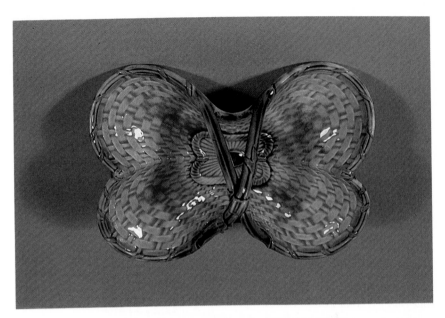

WEDGWOOD BASKET. 8"l. $200.00-250.00.

ETRUSCAN SALT AND PEPPER SHAKERS. 4"h. This pair is in the coral pattern. Impressed L15. $400.00-495.00 for the pair.

GEORGE JONES ANGELS ON DOLPHINS. 7″h. Each holds a swirl pattern-
ed shell. $400.00-450.00 the pair.

CHICK TOOTHPICK. 4″h. $150.00-175.00.

ETRUSCAN TUMBLER. 4"h. This rare Etruscan piece has a pattern very similar to the one on the Baseball Players pitcher, minus the players. Look for a large pitcher in this pattern as well. $150.00-195.00.

MARKS

1. TENUOUS MAJOLICA. This is the mark on the bottom of the very rare Tenuous Majolica shell cuspidor. It is believed that the mark is American.

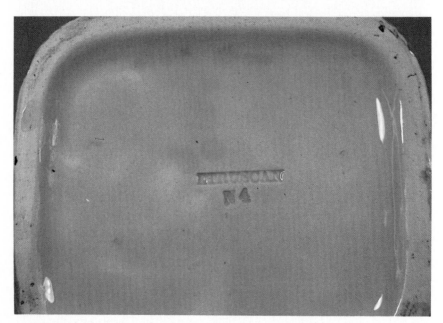

2. ETRUSCAN MARK. This is a variation of the Etruscan mark which appears on the bottom of the rare Etruscan sardine box. For other more common Etruscan marks, please refer to the Marks section of my first book.

Periodicals

Maine Antiques Digest, Waldoboro, Maine   (published 11 times each year)

Ohio Antiques Review, Worthington, Ohio   (published 11 times each year)

Antiques and Arts Weekly, Newtown, Connecticut   (52 issues a year)

Schroeder's Insider, Paducah, Kentucky   (published 12 times each year)

Books

Emmerling, Mary, *American Country - A Style and Source Book,* Clarkson N. Potter Inc.

Gould, Mary Earle, *Early American Wooden Ware,* Tuttle.

Kassay, John, *The Book of Shaker Furniture,* U. of Massachusetts Press.

Pain, Howard, *The Heritage of Country Furniture,* Van Nostrand Reinhold.

Raycraft, Don and Carol, *Wallace-Homestead Price Guide to American Country Antiques,* Wallace-Homestead.

The Rush Light Club, *Early Lighting: A Pictorial Guide.*

Teleki, Gloria, *Baskets of Rural America,* E.P. Dutton.

Webster, Donald Blake, *Decorated Stoneware Pottery of North America,* Tuttle.